Shaquille O'Neal

By Pohla Smith and Steve Wilson

A *Sports Illustrated For Kids* Book

Shaquille O'Neal by Pohla Smith and Steve Wilson

SPORTS ILLUSTRATED FOR KIDS and **KIDS** are registered trademarks of Time Inc.

Cover design by Emily Peterson Perez
Cover photograph by John W. McDonough/Sports Illustrated
Research by Linda Marsch and Steve Pittman

Copyright © 1996, 2000 Time Inc. All rights reserved.

No part of this book may be reproduced or transmitted in any form or by any means, electronic or mechanical, including photocopying, recording, or by any information storage and retrieval system, without permission in writing from the publisher.

Shaquille O'Neal is published by SPORTS ILLUSTRATED FOR KIDS, a division of Time Inc. Its trademark is registered in the U.S. Patent and Trademark Office and in other countries. SPORTS ILLUSTRATED FOR KIDS, 135 West 50th St., New York, NY 10020-1393

If you purchased this book without a cover, you should be aware that this book is stolen property. It was reported as "unsold and destroyed" to the publisher, and neither the author nor the publisher has received any payment for this "stripped" book.

ISBN 1-930623-13-5

Printed in the United States of America

10 9 8 7 6 5 4 3 2 1

Shaquille O'Neal is a production of SPORTS ILLUSTRATED FOR KIDS Books: Cathrine Wolf, Assistant Managing Editor; Emily Peterson Perez, Art Director; Margaret Sieck, Senior Editor; Aaron Derr (Project Editor), Associate Editor; Kathleen Fieffe, Reporter; Robert J. Rohr, Copy Manager; Erin Tricarico, Photo Researcher; Ron Beuzenburg, Production Manager

CONTENTS

1 Superhero at Center 4

2 Army Life 10

3 High School Highlights 18

4 Tiger Time 24

5 Magic Man 31

6 Famous 37

7 Summer School 43

8 Hello, L.A. 51

9 Ring of Champions 56

1
Superhero at Center

The date was June 19, 2000. The setting was Game 6 of the NBA Finals at Staples Center, Los Angeles. The center of attention was Shaquille O'Neal, All-Star big man for the Los Angeles Lakers.

This was it. With a victory over the Indiana Pacers, the 7' 1", 315-pound center would make his biggest dream come true. He was 28 years old, and this was his eighth season as a professional. During that time, he had done almost everything but achieve his number-one goal: winning a National Basketball Association title.

Shaquille had been waiting almost his whole life for this night — at least ever since he decided, at age 13, that he was going to get serious about basketball. Now, 15 years later, Shaq was at the top of his game. His team was tops in the league throughout the 1999-2000 season. He knew this would be his best shot at a championship ring, and he knew also that time was running out on his dream.

Yes, Shaq already had been honored as one of The 50 Greatest Players in NBA History. But he knew as well as anyone that to be mentioned with such all-time great centers as Wilt Chamberlain, Bill Russell, and Kareem Abdul-Jabbar, he had to win at least one NBA title.

Shaq had millions of fans pulling for him. Even people who didn't usually watch basketball knew about him and wanted to see him win it all. Shaq became famous when he left college, in 1992, to turn pro. In fact, he was one of the NBA's most popular players, especially after the retirement of Michael Jordan.

Shaq flashed his big smile on television frequently in soft-drink and shoe commercials. He appeared on late-night talk shows. He was on the cover of *Sports Illustrated*, *GQ*, and *Rolling Stone* magazines. He was written about in newspapers such as *USA Today*, *The Washington Post*, *The Christian Science Monitor*, and *The Village Voice*.

With all that attention came pressure. But if any player could handle it all, it was Shaq. He has always compared himself to Superman, the Man of Steel. Shaq even has a tattoo of Superman's *S* on his left arm.

Before the 1999-2000 season, there were still some goals that Shaq had not reached. He played in All-Star

Games; he won a scoring title, and he won a gold medal at the 1996 Olympics. But he had never been named Most Valuable Player in the NBA. And in his only trip to the Finals, in 1995 when he played with the Orlando Magic, his team lost to Hakeem Olajuwon's Houston Rockets. A pulled stomach muscle hurt his play for two seasons. But in 1999-2000, Shaq played like the Man of Steel throughout the regular season and the playoffs, all the way up to Game 6 of the Finals.

He was a man on a mission. He knew this was his best chance to win the title. He was at his peak, and the entire Laker team was playing great. Their new head coach, Phil Jackson, had coached the Chicago Bulls to six championships. Guard Kobe Bryant, just 21 years old, was showing the stuff of superstardom. High-scoring Glen Rice had been acquired during the 1998-99 season, and the team had solid role players in ex-Bull guard Ron Harper, forward Robert Horry, and point guard Derek Fisher.

"I'm trying to be focused this season," Shaquille said of his attitude going into 1999-2000. "I'm getting older. My window is getting slimmer and slimmer."

Shaq displayed his win-at-all-costs attitude in the 2000 All-Star Game, in Oakland, California. After sharing MVP honors with San Antonio Spur forward Tim Duncan, Shaq wasn't satisfied. "This award is very nice, but I'm trying to get the big-picture award (the NBA title)."

The big man showed his determination in a March 20, 2000, clash with Alonzo Mourning's Miami Heat. Alonzo had emerged as one of the top centers in the Eastern Conference, and the Heat was one of the best teams in the league. In 1998-99, Alonzo had beaten out Shaq for All-NBA first-team honors. Shaq and the Lakers rolled into Miami with one goal for that March game: beat the Heat and prove which is the best team in the league. The two centers went toe-to-toe in a battle of heavyweights. Shaq won the battle by blocking Mourning's shots four times in four minutes during the third quarter. The Lakers rallied to win the war, 100–89.

At the end of the regular season, Shaq ran away with MVP honors. He received 120 of 121 possible first-place votes. No player had won the award by a bigger margin, not even Michael Jordan! Shaquille won the scoring crown with an average of 29.7 points per game. He led the NBA in field-goal percentage (.574) and was second in rebounding (13.6 a game) and third in blocks (3.03 a game).

But his biggest impact came in the standings. Shaq led the Lakers to a league-best 67–15 record. Just five teams in history have done better. His amazing season was just a warm-up for the playoffs. Behind their steamrolling Shaq diesel truck, the Lakers beat the tough Sacramento Kings in the first round.

The Phoenix Suns were the next playoff victim. Then

Shaq and the Lakers triumphed over the Portland Trail Blazers in a close seven-game series to win the Western Conference Finals. Next came the Pacers in the NBA Finals. Powered by their two stars, Superman Shaq and Boy Wonder Kobe, the Lakers won the first two games at Staples Center, in Los Angeles. Back in Indiana, the Pacers took Game 3. The Lakers rebounded to steal the next game in OT, but Indiana wouldn't roll over. Reggie Miller and Jalen Rose led the Pacers to victory in Game 5, and the series returned to Los Angeles with the Lakers leading three games to two. They needed just one more win.

On the night of June 19, 2000, greatness was within Shaq's grasp. He wanted the title for himself, but he also wanted it for his teammates and all their fans. He had spent the last 15 years working toward an NBA title. This was the reason he left the Orlando Magic and came to the Lakers four years ago. When Shaq was a kid, his dad had coached him in basketball. He had given Shaq a great motto with which to psych himself up: "YOUR BALL, YOUR COURT, YOUR GAME!"

The buzzer sounded to start the game. Indiana kept it close until the fourth quarter. That's when Shaq turned his game up another notch. He finished with 41 points, 12 rebounds, and 4 blocked shots. Lakers 116, Pacers 111. The Lakers won the series, 4–2. Shaq capped his dream season with MVP honors for the playoffs. "I've never seen anybody dominate like that, ever," exclaimed Jerry Buss, the Lakers' owner.

Now, like the other great centers, Shaquille O'Neal had his ring.

"It's everything I thought it would be," Shaq said with a huge smile. "Now that we got one, we just have to work on two, three, four, five."

After the playoffs, he would get a three-year, $88.5 million contract extension that would pretty much lock him up as a Laker for the rest of his career. That's just how Shaq wanted it.

Finally, after eight seasons, it was his ball, his court, and his game. He wasn't about to let go. Someone would have to take them from him.

Shaq won his first NBA title in 2000.

Army Life

Shaquille Rashaun O'Neal was born March 6, 1972. He weighed 7 pounds 11 ounces, which isn't that big for a baby. Shaq's mother, Lucille O'Neal, was tall — 6' 2" inches — but her son's birth weight didn't give her any reason to think he would grow up to be a seven-footer!

Lucille liked the sound of that birth weight, anyway. In some dice games, 7 and 11 are lucky numbers, so she was always telling Shaq how lucky they were.

Shaq's mom may have figured her son would need all the luck he could get. They lived in a poor neighborhood in a big, run-down section of Newark, New Jersey. Newark is located 15 miles west of New York City.

Shaquille and his mother didn't have much. Lucille became pregnant with Shaq soon after she finished high school. Shaq's biological father never married his mother.

Lucille gave her baby a special name. Shaquille and Rashaun are Islamic, or Muslim, names. Lucille wasn't Islamic, nor did she follow the Islamic religion. Still, an Islamic group of African Americans, called Black Muslims or the Nation of Islam, had had a good influence on many neighborhoods of Newark. The Muslims urged African Americans to take pride in themselves. They encouraged kids to stay in school. They told kids and adults alike to stay away from drugs and alcohol.

The word *shaquille* means "little one." The word *rashaun* means "warrior." Together, Shaq's name means "little warrior." At least half the name is right!

When Shaq was 2 years old, his mother married Philip Harrison. The two had met when they both worked for the city of Newark. Philip had played junior college and college basketball before he quit school to join the army.

Shaq kept his mother's last name. Lucille and Phil wanted the boy to carry on the O'Neal family name because Lucille had no brothers or nephews. Years later, when Shaq was 21, a man who claimed to be Shaq's real father went on a TV show and told his story. He said he wanted to see Shaq. Shaq said no.

When reporters asked Shaq about it, he said, "Just because you bring a child into the world doesn't make you a father. . . .When my mother needed someone 21 years ago, Phil Harrison was the man. He is my dad. He's the one who raised me and made me what I am today."

When Shaq was old enough to go to school, the family moved to Jersey City. They lived in a big, seven-room house owned by Lucille's mother, Odessa. In his autobiography, *Shaq Attaq!*, published in 1993, Shaq said he thought the house was spooky. He also hated the fact that his school was just across the street!

Then the army transferred his dad to another base, in Bayonne, New Jersey. The family moved into housing right on the base. The family never stayed in one place for long. Mr. Harrison had decided to make a career out of the army. He eventually became a supply sergeant, and the army transferred him, as it does most soldiers, from base to base about every two years. The Harrison family continued to live on army bases until Shaq went away to college.

Shaq's family grew as they moved around. His sister, Lateefah, was born when he was 5. Another sister,

Ayesha, was born a year later. His baby brother, Jamal Harrison, was born a year after Ayesha. (Jamal enrolled in 2000 as a basketball player at Louisiana State University, where Shaq played in college.)

When Shaq was in sixth grade, the family moved across the Atlantic Ocean to Germany. The Harrisons lived on an army base in the mountains, in a town called Wildflecken. They moved back to New Jersey once, then returned to Germany. When Shaq was entering 11th grade, they moved to San Antonio, Texas.

Moving so often had good points and bad points. The good points were that Shaq and his sisters and brother got to see different parts of the United States and Europe. They learned to make friends and adjust to change quickly. The bad points were not having the same friends for long. It seemed every time Shaq got to be a good friend with someone, it was time to pack up and leave again. "I didn't ever really have a best friend," he once said.

Making friends wasn't easy for Shaq. He was so much bigger than most kids his age. By the time he was 13, Shaq was 6' 5" and still growing! "We'd buy him pants on Saturday and by the next Friday, they wouldn't fit," his dad has said with a smile.

Shaq needed time to get used to his big body. He was clumsy. Rude kids made fun of him. Some said he must be a lot older than he said and that he was trying to cover up the fact that he had flunked a grade.

Kids also made fun of Shaq's name. Because it was different, they would call him things like Sasquatch. Now that Shaq is an adult, he is glad he has a special name. But when he was a kid, he wished his name was Tom or Joe. Because kids teased him, Shaq got into a lot of fights. That made other kids think he was mean, which made it even harder to make friends.

Shaq says that fighting was just one of many bad things he did during those first few years the family was moving around. "I really don't know why I was such a bad kid," Shaq says in *Shaq Attaq!* "There was always a lot of love in our house, but it didn't seem to be enough for me. I was always trying to get attention, and so I acted like a juvenile delinquent."

Once, as a little kid, when he was living in his grandmother's house, Shaq set his teddy bear on fire. Luckily, no one was hurt. Another time, he pulled a fire alarm on the army base in Bayonne, New Jersey. The military police hauled him in until his father came and got him.

Shaq misbehaved in class. He threw spitballs and talked out of turn. He got down on the floor and started break-dancing just about any time he felt like it. He wanted to be a professional dancer. He was very good at dancing, even though he was big. But the classroom was not the place.

Every time Shaq's parents found out he had been bad, they punished him. For a long time, it made no difference.

Shaq misbehaved the most when his family first arrived in Germany. He started hanging out with army kids whose fathers were commissioned officers (Philip Harrison was not an officer). The other kids' dads made more money, and they had nicer things than Shaq. He felt jealous.

At first, Shaq hated Germany. He missed the United States. The rumor among the army kids was that if a kid didn't behave, he would get sent back home. Shaq decided he would be so bad, his mom and dad would send him back.

His parents finally figured out what he was doing. Shaq remembers his dad sitting down with him for a talk one day. Mr. Harrison said, "Look, son, no matter what you do, I'm not letting them send you back." He also told Shaq he would continue to punish Shaq every time he misbehaved.

"One time, my parents punished me for a whole year," Shaq said once. "All I could do was go to school and come home."

As bad as he was, there were some things Shaq would not do. "I will say with some pride that I never got into drugs and alcohol," Shaq says. He was afraid — as he should have been — that drugs would kill him. When he tasted beer for the first time, he hated it.

Shaq at last began to get the message from his

parents. It happened when he was about 13. "I finally got tired of being punished and tried it their way," he says. "And it worked." He began behaving in class. He walked away from fights. He listened more closely to his teachers. He discovered that he didn't have to be bad to get attention.

Shaq says that what helped most in turning him into a better kid was sports. His dad had been a good athlete, and he taught Shaq football and basketball. He even coached some of the teams Shaq played on.

Although he was very big, Shaq was a tailback on army-base football teams. He was a scary sight on the field! He finally quit football when he moved to Germany because he got tired of smaller kids chopping him in the knees.

As big as he was, basketball did not come easily to Shaq. A lot of big kids just stand under the basket, catch passes, and make easy shots. But Mr. Harrison didn't let his son take the easy way out. He wanted Shaq to learn real basketball skills. For example, Mr. Harrison taught him how to make accurate passes to teammates.

There was another reason basketball was tough for Shaq. He had a disorder in his knees called Osgood-Schlatter's disease, which affects growing joints. It is painful, and Shaq's knees hurt a lot.

To treat the disease, he had to take a lot of calcium — the mineral that builds strength in bones. He took calcium pills and drank a lot of milk.

Shaq says the disease made it hard for him to improve quickly in basketball. He didn't jump well. It took him a long time to learn to dunk, even though he was already about 6' 7." The coach cut him from the team when he was in ninth grade. He said Shaq's feet were too big and he was too clumsy.

In his autobiography, Shaq tells a touching story about his first dunk: "One day it just happened. It was a real weak dunk but it was a dunk, and I ran off the court yelling to all my friends to come watch me dunk."

You can guess what happened when all his buddies came to watch: He couldn't do it!

Despite these frustrations, it was clear that Shaq had everything it takes to be a good basketball player: size, strength, coordination and rhythm, and the self-control to work hard and improve. Eventually, it would all come together.

High School Highlights

By the time Shaq finally learned to dunk, he had already seen what doors basketball might open for him. When Shaq was 13, he attended a basketball clinic on the army base in Germany, where he was living. The head basketball coach at Louisiana State University, Dale Brown, gave the clinic.

Shaq remembers Coach Brown talking about shooting. He told the people in the audience that arm position was the key to good shooting. Then he looked for someone in the crowd to try shooting the way he said. Shaq got up and took a shot. The ball hit the rim, but it didn't go in. Shaq remembers the coach saying "Good shot."

That made Shaq feel brave. After the clinic, he told Coach Brown he had bad knees and couldn't jump well enough to dunk. He asked the coach to show him some exercises that would make his legs stronger. Coach Brown told him about a basic exercise program he could do with weight-training equipment. Then Coach Brown asked Shaquille how long he had been in the army.

"I'm not in the army. I'm only 13," Shaq said. Coach Brown was shocked. He asked Shaq if he was playing on a school team. Shaq explained he wasn't good enough. The coach then asked Shaq what size shoes he wore. When Shaq told him he wore size 17, Coach Brown got excited. He realized that those big feet meant Shaq might become a 7-footer! Coach Brown, like many college basketball coaches, was always looking for 7-footers who could play the game.

Coach Brown asked to meet Shaq's father. He told Mr. Harrison that Shaq probably would grow to be more than seven feet. If he became good enough at basketball, he could get a college scholarship. In fact, Coach Brown would love to have Shaq play for Louisiana State.

Shaq may have been impressed, but Mr. Harrison wasn't. He interrupted Coach Brown before he could finish. Shaq wrote about that meeting in his book. His dad said, "Coach, I'm not trying to be rude. But I'm not interested in hearing about basketball. Tell me about how you want to help my son make something of himself beyond basketball." Coach

Brown was impressed by Mr. Harrison's concerns. The two men decided to keep in touch.

Meanwhile, Shaq kept working on his game, trying to become a stronger, better athlete. "I don't believe in talent. I believe in working hard," Shaq said after he had grown up.

Even as a teenager, he worked hard. His dad helped him. Shaq exercised to make his knees, ankles, and thighs strong. His father taught him basketball moves he had learned in college. Shaq worked on ball handling. He worked on jumping for rebounds. He worked on how to be in the right place to get a loose ball.

"I learned how to never give up. I just kept practicing every day," Shaq said. "When everybody was going to parties, I was outside dribbling, working on my coordination, and trying to dunk."

The hard work paid off. He grew stronger and gained coordination. He learned to dunk. And when he was in the 10th grade, he made the team at the high school on the base in Germany.

The following spring, in 1987, when Shaquille was 15, the Harrisons returned to the U.S., to a base called Fort Sam Houston, in San Antonio, Texas. Shaq enrolled as a junior in Robert G. Cole Senior High School. When basketball practice started, he made the team! In fact, Shaquille, now 6' 9", quickly became a star.

The coach at Cole, Dave Madura, was impressed by what he saw. "A lot of kids come in from Germany, and they have these big stats that don't mean anything," Coach Madura said. "Shaq, though, could do everything he said he could do."

Shaq wore jersey number 33, the same number Kareem Abdul-Jabbar wore with the Los Angeles Lakers. Kareem was one of Shaq's heroes. Julius Erving, the high-flying forward known as Doctor J, was another.

With Shaq leading the team at center, the Cole Cougars were undefeated during the regular season. They went to the Texas state playoffs. There they won their semi-final game and took a 32–0 season record into the state championship game, against Liberty Hill High School.

Shaq was cocky because there was nobody on Liberty Hill's team taller than 6' 3". Shaq was *too* confident. In a TV interview, he boasted, "I'm going to score fifty points. Nobody on Earth can stop me." Shaq even stayed out late the night before the game.

The Liberty Hill players showed that size wasn't everything. They made long jump shot after long jump shot, and Shaq couldn't stop them. He became frustrated. He committed four fouls in the first two minutes! He had to sit out the rest of the quarter to avoid the risk of fouling out. While he sat on the bench, Liberty Hill took a 21–2 lead.

Though Shaq made just 8 points in the game, his teammates fought back. They closed to within 1 point with five seconds left in the game. Shaq was fouled and awarded two free throws. The Cole Cougars would win if Shaq made the shots. He missed them both!

"That was the last time I ever said I was bigger than anyone," Shaq said later.

By this time, even after that poor performance, Coach Brown was not the only scout or coach interested in Shaq. Coaches from all over the U.S. were writing to Shaq or visiting him to say they'd like him to play for them after he graduated from high school.

Shaq had a list of four schools he thought about attending. In the end, Shaq decided he wanted to play for Coach Brown at Louisiana State. Coach Brown had kept in touch with Shaq after they had met in Germany. When Shaq's family moved back to Texas, Coach Brown sometimes came to watch him play. Shaq knew Coach Brown had believed in him even when he was a gawky 13-year-old.

Shaq signed with LSU in November. Some people thought Shaq's father had made the decision for him. But Mr. Harrison told reporters he had allowed Shaq to make his own choice.

"We told him, 'Go out there and take what we taught you and what you have learned in life and apply it to do what you have to do,'" he said.

At the time of the signing, Mr. Harrison promised Coach Brown that his son wouldn't leave college to turn professional before he graduated. "If blacks are to get a piece of the American pie, we should get an education," Mr. Harrison said.

Before Shaq headed off to college, he had two things to do first: finish his senior year in high school and lead his team to the state title they had lost the year before. He did just that. The Cole Cougars had a 36–0 season and won the state title! Shaq scored an average of more than 32 points per game — and earned his high school diploma.

Shaq was named a high school All-America. He also was invited to play in the McDonald's High School All-America Game, in Kansas City, Missouri. That game features the best high school players in the nation. Shaq scored 18 points and grabbed 16 rebounds. He also amazed fans by going coast-to-coast on one play. The big guy grabbed a rebound on defense, dribbled the ball all the way to the other end, and dunked.

Shaq attack!

Tiger Time

In the fall of 1989, Shaquille left for his freshman year at Louisiana State University with high hopes. Every college player hopes to play in the NCAA tournament, the Final Four, and maybe even the national championship game. Shaq had reason to believe he would get there with the LSU Tigers. Maybe even as a freshman!

Louisiana State was fortunate enough to have two other very good players: sophomore guard Chris Jackson and 7-foot sophomore Stanley Roberts, who played center and forward. The Tigers also had a great coach in Dale Brown. At least one national sports magazine picked LSU to win the NCAA championship that season.

Shaq was studying business. He wanted to have a back-up career in case he didn't make it as a basketball player. If he did make it in the pros, he figured he could use some of the business skills he learned to manage his own money.

But the big freshman's first order of business was to get

used to college life. He lived in a dormitory with other students. It wasn't glamorous. For example, there were no private bathrooms. Shaq had never lived away from home before. He became homesick. He called home a lot. He also drove home as many weekends as possible, even though it took seven hours to drive from LSU, in Baton Rouge, Louisiana, to San Antonio, Texas.

Once basketball season started, Shaq couldn't go home on weekends. But when the Tigers played a home game, Shaq's family drove to Baton Rouge to watch him play.

Shaquille learned quickly that college basketball was a lot harder than high school ball. LSU plays in the Southeast Conference (SEC). The SEC is one of the best basketball conferences in the nation. Every year, at least a couple of SEC teams are among the 64 colleges that qualify for the NCAA playoffs.

Playing in such a tough conference meant that Shaq could no longer count on being the best player in the game. The players he and his teammates went up against were all good. Offensively, Shaq found it harder to score. And on defense, he committed a lot of fouls.

As the basketball season got under way, the team wasn't playing as a unit. Many of the Tiger players, including point guard Chris Jackson, would shoot whenever they could, instead of looking to pass to a teammate who might have a better shot. Chris was scoring an average of 28 points per game. Stanley Roberts was the second-leading scorer with 14 points.

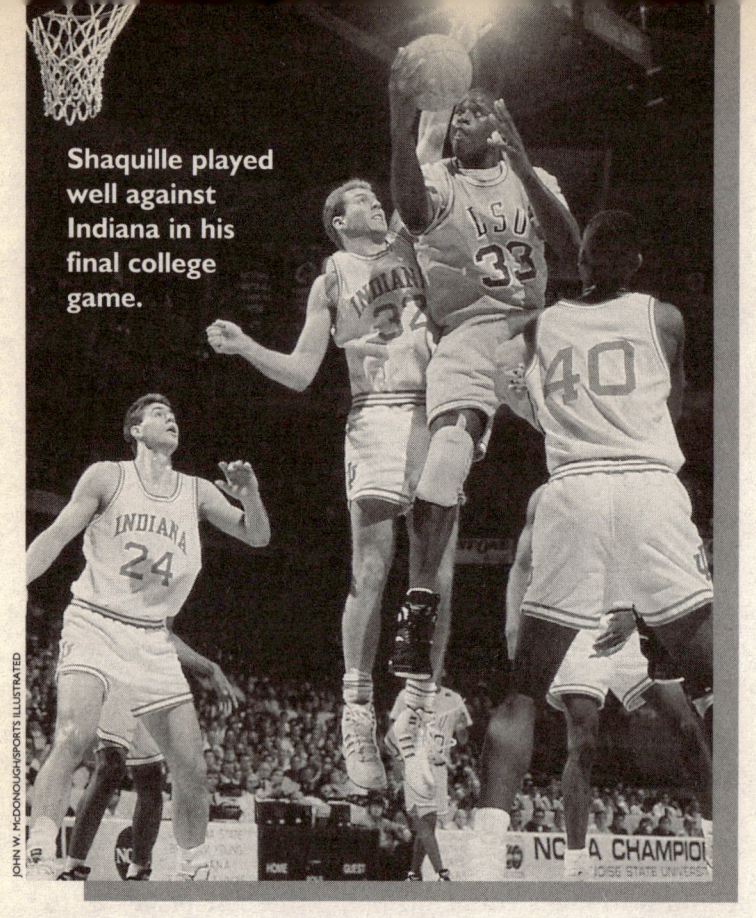

Shaquille played well against Indiana in his final college game.

Shaq didn't shoot that often, but he shot well. He ended the season with a scoring average of 13.9 points per game. He also averaged about 12 rebounds per game. That was good enough for Shaq to be named to the All-Southeastern Conference team and a freshman All-America.

The Tigers had a 23–9 record during the regular season. In the NCAA tournament, they won their first game but lost the second one. Everyone was disappointed.

After the season, Chris and Stanley left college to turn pro. When Shaq returned to LSU for his sophomore year, in 1990, everyone knew that it was time for him to take charge of the team's offense. In some polls, the Tigers were picked to finish fifth or sixth in their conference. But Shaq blossomed in his new role. During one nationally televised game, against the University of Arizona, in December, he scored 29 points, grabbed 14 rebounds, blocked 6 shots, made 5 steals — and, since he had been in early foul trouble, he didn't even play the whole game!

Shaq benefited from some special private lessons that year. Coach Brown arranged for two of the best centers in NBA history to work with him. Bill Walton, who had starred for the Portland Trail Blazers in the late 1970's, worked with Shaq on passing, footwork, and avoiding foul trouble. To help Shaq improve his jump shots and hook shots, Coach Brown turned to one of Shaq's original heroes, Kareem Abdul-Jabbar.

Thanks to Shaq, LSU went 20–10. But then, bad luck struck. Shaq broke his left leg playing Florida just before the regular season ended. He missed the last game and the SEC playoffs. Without their big guy, the Tigers lost both games.

When LSU was invited to the NCAA tournament, Shaq tried to play in the game against the University of

Connecticut. It was obvious that his leg still bothered him, and Connecticut won, 79–62.

It was disappointing for Shaq and the team to go home so soon. Still, Shaq had proven a lot that year. He became the first player to lead the SEC in all the following categories: scoring (27.6 points per game), rebounding (14.7 per game), field-goal percentage (62.8 percent), and blocked shots (140). He also led the entire nation in rebounding, and his average of five blocks per game was an NCAA record for a sophomore.

With numbers like those, Shaq was named the SEC Player of the Year and a first-team All-America. He received the Adolph Rupp Award from the Associated Press. The trophy, named after the University of Kentucky coaching legend, is given to the player voted best in the nation.

Because he was attracting so much attention, people started asking Shaq if he was going to leave school and turn pro. But Shaq's parents said no. They wanted Shaq to be the first person in their families to get a college degree.

Shaq's dad, Mr. Harrison, said, "The money will be there when you're ready."

When the 1991-92 season began, expectations for the team's success were much higher than they had been the year before. The Tigers had two new players, Jamie Brandon and Clarence Ceasar, who were good outside shooters. Teams had to concentrate on players other than Shaq now. The Tigers were ranked Number 6 in the country during the pre-season.

The ranking didn't last. LSU started out slowly. Again, the players weren't playing as a team. Shaq was still getting double- and triple-teamed. He was frustrated, and he said so.

People started criticizing him. They said he was playing conservatively so that he wouldn't get hurt or so that he wouldn't be charged with personal fouls. Even his family yelled at him. When he went home for Christmas, his dad made him watch videos of his games. He scolded Shaq for "playing too nice." Even one of Shaq's grandmothers called from New Jersey and criticized him.

Shaq listened to his family. When he went back to school in January, he played harder. His statistics improved: He scored more than 24 points per game, and he led the nation in rebounds and blocks.

LSU finished the regular season with a 19–8 record overall and 10–3 in the SEC. The Tigers went on to the SEC tournament determined to win it.

In a first-round game against Tennessee, Shaq lost his temper while getting shoved around. He got into a fight. Soon everybody on both teams was involved. Shaquille and a Tennessee player were thrown out, and Shaq was suspended for the next game. Without Shaq, LSU lost in the second round.

At the NCAA tournament, Shaq was determined to

make the most of another opportunity to win an NCAA title for LSU and his coach. LSU beat Brigham Young in the first round. Unfortunately, the Tigers' second-round opponent was Indiana University, one of the best teams in the tournament. It was an experienced team. Indiana's coach, Bobby Knight, was considered to be one of the best coaches in the country.

Shaq had a great game against the Indiana Hoosiers. He scored 36 points, made 12 rebounds, and blocked 5 shots. But a one-man effort wasn't good enough to win. Indiana whipped the Tigers, 89–79.

Though they didn't know it yet, fans had seen Shaq play his last college game. A few days after the loss to Indiana, Shaq drove home to San Antonio. While he was driving, he decided he was ready to leave school and turn pro. At home, he told his parents about his decision. He explained that he was leaving because he felt he could not grow anymore as a player in college. He also promised to go back and get his degree during the off-seasons.

Shaq had had a good college basketball career. Over three seasons, he scored an average of 21.6 points and pulled down 13.5 rebounds per game. Although he had struggled at the beginning of his third and final year, he played well enough to be named SEC Player of the Year and All-America for the second time. Now he was going to have to get ready for the *really* big time.

5
Magic Man

After high school, Shaq could pick which college he attended. But he couldn't pick which pro team he would play for. The NBA has a draft, and teams pick the players.

The Orlando Magic had the first pick. The Magic had had a record of 21 wins and 61 losses in the season just ended. Their longest winning streak had been three games in a row, and their longest losing streak was 17 games! The team needed help.

On June 24, 1992, the NBA held its draft at Memorial Coliseum, in Portland, Oregon. The Orlando Magic went first and picked Shaquille, who was at the Coliseum, talking to reporters. At the same time, back in Orlando, about 8,000 fans who had gathered in Orlando Arena for a draft-Shaq party were yelling and screaming. Another big crowd turned out at the Orlando Airport to greet Shaq.

But the Magic isn't the only big attraction in the Orlando area. Just a short drive from the team's home court is another Magic Kingdom — Walt Disney

World. When Shaq got off the plane, he was wearing Mickey Mouse ears. The fans really liked that.

Shaq told his agent, Leonard Armato, to negotiate a contract with Orlando quickly. Sometimes rookie players and their new teams can't agree on contracts. The rookies end up being holdouts and can't practice with their teams. Shaq told Leonard he didn't want to hold out. He said he didn't need any fancy clauses guaranteeing he would be the highest-paid player in the league.

Leonard negotiated a contract that guaranteed the Magic would pay Shaq about $40 million over seven years. Shaq signed his contract on August 5, 1992. That was the earliest an NBA rookie had signed a contract in 11 years!

Shaq worked hard to get ready for the season. He found an apartment in Los Angeles, California, and started playing pickup basketball with NBA players, as well as recently retired Laker star Magic Johnson. Shaq learned a lot playing against Magic and others like Houston Rocket center Hakeem Olajuwon.

Shaq and Hakeem worked out together at Inglewood High School, near Los Angeles. Shaq wrote about the experience in *Shaq Attaq!*: "Hakeem showed me some moves. He told me what he does in certain situations, and we just talked. If you want to compare me to any athlete, compare me to Hakeem. He's a great player and a hard worker, but off the court he's a class act. I think he's the best center in the league." Shaq also liked the way Hakeem dressed and the polite, friendly way he acted off the court.

That summer, Shaq went to a basketball camp for top players. It is called Pete Newell's Big Man's Camp. Pete has worked with many NBA players. He helped Shaq develop more polished moves.

Finally, Orlando's training camp began in October. Shaq did well. One of the hardest things he had to do was run for 12 minutes. He had to be fast enough to cover a mile in the first seven minutes. Although Shaq's a 315-pound guy, he ran the first mile in 6 minutes 45 seconds. To help Shaq get ready to play against top NBA centers, the Magic invited center Mark McNamara to camp.

Mark spent a lot of time working with Shaq. Greg Kite, Shaq's backup

In Orlando, Shaq was as popular as Mickey Mouse.

with the Magic, was a veteran like Mark and tried to show Shaq what the NBA would be like.

The first couple of weeks of camp went fast. Before Shaq knew it, it was time for his first exhibition games. Shaq was nervous. In his autobiography, he says he had "butterflies as big as buzzards."

The first game was against the Miami Heat. It was obvious that Shaq was nervous. He made nine turnovers. But Shaq did some good things in the game, too: He scored 25 points while making 11 of 16 shots playing against center Rony Seikaly, a former star at Syracuse University. He also had six rebounds and blocked three shots.

That was the way the rest of the exhibition season went. Shaq made mistakes. He had a lot of turnovers and personal fouls, and often his free-throw shooting was terrible. But for the most part, he did more good things than bad. He finished the eight-game exhibition season with averages of 17.8 points and 10 rebounds per game, the best numbers on the team. He also led the Magic in blocks with 15 and steals with 10.

Now he felt ready to play the games that counted. And the 13,000 people who had bought season tickets to Magic games were ready to see him play. They were anxious to see a Shaq attack! Shaq didn't disappoint them: He attacked opponents. Through the first five regular-season games, in November 1992, he led the league in rebounding (16.4 per game), and was fourth in scoring (25.8) and fifth in blocked shots (3.4). The Magic won three of those games. Shaq played so well that the NBA named him Player of the Week. He was the first rookie ever to win the honor. Shaq stayed hot almost all the way through November, and his heat made his teammates play better.

The Magic won eight of its first 11 games and was first in the Atlantic Division in the Eastern Conference. Shaq was named NBA Player of the Week for the second week of November and then NBA Player of the Month! He was the first rookie to win that honor.

No team stays hot forever — especially playing as often as NBA teams play. The NBA regular season is 82 games long — about three times as many as Shaq played in a college season. Sometimes teams play two games in two days. They also spend several days away on road trips, traveling in planes and sleeping in hotel rooms. A player can get tired, especially if he's not used to that pace. Shaq, like other rookies, found the playing schedule in the NBA tougher than it had been in college.

The players Shaq was facing were also much better than those he had played against in college, and the defenses were different. The players Shaq went up against in the NBA were more physical. There was a lot of grabbing and holding that Shaq found difficult to get used to.

The Magic cooled off in December in a big way.

Orlando lost its first six games that month and fell out of first place in the Atlantic Division. Shaq learned from the losses, too. He learned that because the season is long, he can't worry too much about losing streaks. The Magic followed its six losses with four straight victories — the longest winning streak in the young team's history.

In February, Shaq made headlines in a nationally televised game at Phoenix against the Suns. He made a sensational dunk early in the game, and the whole backboard came crashing down. Shaq didn't do it on purpose, of course, but it was amazing. It showed how big and strong Shaq is.

The fans voted Shaquille to be the starting center for the East at the annual mid-season All-Star Game, beating out Knick veteran Patrick Ewing. That made Shaq the first rookie to be voted to start an All-Star Game since Michael Jordan in 1985. Shaq had 14 points and seven rebounds in the game.

Shaq finished the season as the team leader in scoring (23.4 points per game), rebounds (13.9 per game), and blocks (3.5 per game). Even though he was a rookie, he was the only player in the NBA to rank in the Top 10 in four different categories. No wonder he was named NBA Rookie of the Year!

Thanks in large part to Shaq, the Magic finished the season with 41 wins and 41 losses, 20 more wins than the season before.

6

Famous

The Magic didn't qualify for the 1992-93 playoffs, but Shaq was on television often during the first weekend of post-season competition: 48 minutes — all in commercials. By that time, even people who didn't follow pro basketball knew who Shaq was.

Shaq appeared in commercials for Reebok and Pepsi-Cola. He had his own line of Kenner toys. He had been on TV talk shows. He had even performed a rap song with his favorite group, Fu Schnickens, on TV. He had his own rap album in the works, and he was going to spend part of the summer making a movie called *Blue Chips*.

Shaq had started to become famous when he was in college. He attracted a lot of attention because he was so big and so talented. When he gave interviews, he came across as an overgrown kid. People felt that if they could get to know him, they'd want him to be their friend. When Shaq was still in college, a couple even named their baby Shaquille O'Neal Long.

Another couple named a female racehorse after him — Shaquilla O'Neala.

Everybody felt that Shaq was going to be a big star once he turned pro and was allowed to endorse products. It started right after the NBA draft. First, Shaq signed a deal with a card company, called Classic Cards, to make a draft-pick trading card. That meant no other companies could have Shaq cards in their draft-pick sets. In six months, Classic Cards sold $25 million worth of their 1992 draft-pick sets featuring Shaq!

Shaq and Leonard Armato, his agent, then talked to sports-shoe companies about having Shaq endorse a shoe. When Shaq first went to visit the people at Reebok, in a suburb of Boston, Massachusetts, they gave him a hero's welcome.

It seemed as if everybody who worked for Reebok was waiting for Shaq in the lobby of the company's building! And all of them were wearing special T-shirts that said WHO'S THE MAN on the front and SHAQ on the back. They gave Shaq a special jacket, too. Once the officers started talking business, they told Shaq they planned to design a special shoe just for him to endorse. They had an idea for a TV commercial in which he'd meet basketball legends like Wilt Chamberlain, Kareem Abdul-Jabbar, and Bill Walton.

After more negotiations, Leonard went back to Reebok. Quickly, he and the company agreed on a big contract. The contract made Shaq a multimillionaire.

Shaq and the basketball legends filmed the Reebok commercials before he left for his rookie training camp. In one, he showed off for the famous retired basketball players and retired UCLA coach John Wooden by making a big dunk that broke the glass backboard. Then the legends put Shaq in his place. They handed him a broom and dustpan so that he could clean up his own mess! It made people see that Shaq wasn't too big to laugh at himself.

Shaq split with Reebok in 1998 and started wearing Chromz, a Dunk brand, sold exclusively on Shaq's website, dunk.com. The site is co-owned by Shaq and his agent, and sells custom athletic shoes and sportswear. Shaq also signed a contract with Kenner toys for a line of action figures. Later, he made deals to represent Pepsi-Cola and a computer-game company. In 1994, he reportedly made $12.5 million just for his product endorsements. In 2000, he signed a contract extension with the Lakers that will pay him an average of $29.5 million per season.

Shaq gets frustrated that the media spend so much time adding up the amounts of money he makes. He's afraid people will think that money is all he thinks about. He talks about that in *Shaq Attaq!*: "I'm not about money. I'm not about seeing how many cars I can buy or how many closets I can fill up with clothes. I make more money in one year than my father made in his entire life, but that doesn't make me a better person than him.

"The bad thing, though, is people assume you've changed because now you have money."

One example of that occurs when people ask Shaq for his autograph. He sometimes asks them to wait until he finishes what he's doing at the moment. At times, they get mad and say he thinks he's too good to sign because he's rich. Shaq doesn't think that's fair.

So far, Shaq doesn't seem to have changed since he became a millionaire. It's true he owns cool cars and a nice house. He wears a lot of jewelry and has a leather coat with a Superman-style *S* on it. He can't go anyplace in public without fans making a big fuss. But, otherwise, his life away from the basketball court or the television cameras isn't much different from that of any young, unmarried guy with a good job.

Shaq is careful about his body. He doesn't drink alcohol. He's usually the designated driver if he goes with friends to nightclubs. When he was drafted by the Orlando Magic, he celebrated by taking a few of his boyhood buddies to a water park near San Antonio, called Splashtown.

For a few years, Shaq shared his big home with a former college teammate, Dennis Tracey, who works as Shaq's assistant. They lived like other young guys. Neither one of them is good at housework, so they had someone come in to clean. Their "cooking" would have given a nutritionist nightmares! Shaq's favorite foods are his mom's fried chicken and macaroni and cheese. He often goes out for fast food. When he doesn't, he uses his microwave to heat frozen food. On the day of a home game, Shaq likes to eat pizza and pasta before he goes to the arena.

When he's not playing basketball, making movies or commercials, or signing autographs, Shaq likes to watch action movies (he has an eight-seat movie theater in his house) and play video games. He also plays with his two Rottweiler dogs, Shazam and Thor.

Shaq wears an earring, and he has a tattoo of the Superman *S* on his left arm and one on his right arm that shows two hands around a globe, accompanied by the initials T.W.IS.M. (THE WORLD IS MINE). He loves to buy wild hats, but it's hard for him to go out shopping without being mobbed by fans.

He likes to play practical jokes. For instance, when he's on the team airplane, Shaq might paint the fingernails of a sleeping teammate!

Shaq is generous. He bought houses for all of his grandparents, and he has set up a fund to provide money for his mother and stepfather as long as they live. He buys presents for his brother and sisters and likes to give presents to his teammates' kids, too! Shaq also likes to do things for people he doesn't know. Sometimes he'll hand out $100 bills to homeless people. If he gets a letter or a telephone call about some little kid in the hospital, he'll try his best to make time to call or visit the kid.

Shaq gets more than 1,000 fan letters each week. At Thanksgiving, Shaq holds "Shaqsgiving." He buys and helps to serve a big Thanksgiving dinner for homeless people. At Christmas, he plays Shaq-a-Claus and buys gifts for poor kids.

A lot of the helpful things Shaq does are directed at kids. For example, he buys season tickets to NBA games every year. Those seats are for the Shaq Paq. Every game, the tickets go to a club or a group of kids who might otherwise never see a game at an NBA arena.

Shaq is donating $15 million over a 10-year span to the Boys & Girls Clubs of America. The donation will fund technology centers in Boys & Girls Clubs nationwide. Each center will be equipped with eight or more computers, including modems, scanners, digital cameras, laser printers, and network computers. Shaq is an alumnus of the Newark (New Jersey) Boys & Girls Club.

Shaq is a spokesman for Reading Is Fundamental and has recorded a video with RIF that encourages kids to read. Shaq likes kids best. He thinks it's because he's still a kid himself. He was only 20 when he started playing pro basketball!

Summer School

Shaq was so busy during the summer after his rookie season that some people criticized him. How could he improve his basketball game when he was filming a movie, recording a rap album, and touring Asia?

But Shaq wasn't as far from basketball as it seemed. The movie, *Blue Chips*, was about basketball, and Shaq played the role of a highly recruited college star. (Does that sound familiar?) Director William Friedkin hired real coaches and real players so that he could film real basketball games. One of the players in the movie was the Magic's newest draft pick, Anferee "Penny" Hardaway.

When he wasn't filming, Shaq worked out with a kick-boxing champion. Those workouts were designed to increase Shaq's flexibility and make his legs stronger.

For the second straight summer, he attended Pete Newell's Big Man's Camp. Later, one of his basketball rivals told reporters what he thought of Shaq's work at the camp.

"Shaq worked as hard as anybody there," said Shawn Kemp, who was a center for the Seattle SuperSonics at the time. "We played against each other a lot, and he's got a lot better skills in the post than a lot of people give him credit for."

Shaq's efforts paid off. In his second season, he played even better than he had as a rookie. For the second straight season, he was the only NBA player to rank in the Top 10 in four categories. He was first in field-goal percentage (.599), second in scoring (29.3 points per game), second in rebounding (13.2 per game), and sixth in blocks (231). He had 286 blocks the previous season, but in his second season, he had 16 more steals and 43 more assists than the year before.

Despite those achievements, Shaq continued to receive criticism during that second season. People seemed to think Shaq was earning too much money too soon and that he didn't work hard enough for it. Tree Rollins disagreed with them. Tree, a 17-year pro who was an assistant coach and backup center to Shaq, said, "He's very receptive to learning, and he wants to learn, which is important."

Still, others criticized him for not being an artful player. They said he relied on his size and strength to score his points off slam-dunks instead of learning to shoot jump shots and hook shots. Shaq responded that opposing defenses concentrated on him. That made it harder for him to take shots other than those powerful dunks, where he just out-muscled players to the basket.

"I have a lot of moves, but it's hard to show them when I have four guys on me," he told one newspaper. "If anybody will play me one-on-one, I'll show you some stuff."

Shaq was fouled often, and often late in the game. The reason? Shaq was a poor free-throw shooter. If opponents wanted to use a personal foul to try to get the ball away from the Magic, Shaq was the best Orlando player to foul. He made only 59 percent of his free throws as a rookie and only 52 percent in his second year. Those numbers were not good. Most NBA players make about 75 percent of their free throws.

"I'm going to get better," Shaq vowed halfway through the season. "I'm still young, still learning. I got surprises they're not ready for yet."

The best answer to all the criticism, though, was not Shaq's statistics or his promises to improve. The best response was Orlando's team statistics. Like its second-year star, the four-year-old franchise had a better season in 1993-94 than it had the prior season. Its record of 50 wins (nine more than the year before) and 32 losses was the best in its history. Better yet, it was good enough for Orlando to finish second in the tough Atlantic Division of the Eastern Conference — right behind the New York Knicks.

The Magic made it into the playoffs for the first time

that year, but they didn't stay long. Orlando faced the Indiana Pacers in the first round of the best-of-five-game series. The Pacers swept the first three games and sent Orlando home for the year.

No one was more disappointed than Shaq. "I know that all the commercials, all the movie roles, all the press stories won't mean anything unless I get a championship," he wrote in his book.

After his second season in the NBA, Shaq once again had a busy summer. He worked on a second rap album and finished a video game. He kept his promise to his parents and went back to Louisiana State University to take classes. (Shaq was expected to graduate from LSU with a degree in General Studies in December 2000.)

Shaq still found time to develop a new weapon in his offense: He perfected a jump hook shot that he could make from as far as 11 feet! He also learned to pass the ball off to a teammate more often when he was swarmed with defenders.

"Just to see the way he's developing is incredible," Houston Rocket center Hakeem Olajuwon said as the 1994-95 season began.

Shaq's young teammates, like second-year guard Penny Hardaway and four-year guard/forward Dennis Scott, were also getting better with experience. Another improvement was the signing of free-agent Horace

Grant, a power forward and tough rebounder who had won three straight NBA championships as Michael Jordan's teammate with the Chicago Bulls.

In the 1994-95 season, Shaq played like a man on a mission. His desire must have been contagious because his teammates played that way, too. Not only did the Magic qualify for the playoffs, but they beat out the New York Knicks to win the Atlantic Division. That was Orlando's first title of any kind.

Shaq, of course, was the Magic's main man. He averaged 29.3 points per game to lead the NBA in scoring. He was third in rebounding with 11.4 per game and sixth in blocks with an average of 2.43. As a team, the Magic scored an average of 110.9 points per game — the most in the NBA.

They finished the season with a record of 57 wins and 25 losses. The Magic played their best in front of the noisy, loyal fans who filled Orlando Arena game after game. Shaq and his teammates lost only two home games.

The only element the Magic lacked as they headed into the playoffs was experience. Except for Horace Grant, the other starters' playoff experience was limited to the three games the team had lost in the first round the year before.

In the NBA, teams usually work several years toward a title, gaining experience and advancing farther in the playoffs each year. The Magic players, however, didn't have a lot of patience. The slogan the team's public relations experts wrote for the playoffs expressed the players' feelings: WHY NOT US? WHY NOT NOW?

The Magic's first assignment in the playoffs was to beat the Boston Celtics in three out of five games. Boston was the eighth and last seed in the Eastern Conference. The Magic won the series in four games.

The second round of playoffs, the Eastern Conference semifinals, was a best-of-seven series. The Magic faced the Michael Jordan-led Chicago Bulls. The Bulls had already won three NBA titles in the 1990's, and Michael had come out of retirement to rejoin the team in time for these playoffs. But Michael was still rusty, and Orlando had the home-court advantage.

The first two games were at Orlando Arena, where each team won once. Then the teams each won a game in Chicago. Back in Orlando, veteran Horace Grant led the way in Game 5. The Magic were up again, three games to two. All they needed was one more win, and they had two games in which to try. Orlando won Game 6, 108–102 . . . and the series!

The Magic's opponent in the Eastern Conference Finals were the Indiana Pacers, the team that had swept Orlando out of the first round in three straight games the year before. Orlando wanted revenge.

In Game 1, in Orlando, Shaq got into early foul trouble, and the Pacers leapt out to a 23–5 lead. But Orlando got back into the game. And when Shaq returned, the Magic were able to win, 104–101.

In Game 2, Shaq scored 39 points to lead Orlando to a 119–114 victory. The Magic lost Games 3 and 4. The two teams returned to Orlando for Game 5. Shaq took charge, scoring a whopping 35 points to lead Orlando to a 108–106 victory. Orlando was back on top, three games to two. But the Pacers hammered the Magic in Game 6, 123–96. The series was tied at three games each, going to the deciding Game 7, in Orlando. The Magic would have the home-court edge, but the Pacers had the experience.

As it turned out, the Magic also had more desire. All five starters scored in double figures — Shaq was the high scorer with 25 — and the defense allowed Indiana to make only 37 percent of its shots. Orlando became Eastern Conference champions with a 105–81 win.

"Maybe we don't have a lot of experience," Magic guard Nick Anderson said. "But we have a lot of heart." That heart showed when the Magic went on to its first NBA championship series against Hakeem Olajuwon and the Houston Rockets.

The series opened with a tough loss for the Magic. Orlando was full of hopes and desire. It took an early 57–37 lead. But the defending champions bounced back. The Magic's lead disappeared, and the Rockets won in overtime on a game-winning tip-in by Hakeem.

Hakeem praised Shaq after the game. "I'm so sore right now," Hakeem said. "Shaquille is so physical and hard to guard. . . . He's my toughest opponent."

The loss was hard for the Magic to recover from, and

Houston rolled to a 117–106 victory in Game 2. Shaq scored 33 points and had 12 rebounds and 7 assists. But the Rockets got 34 points from Hakeem.

The series moved to The Summit, in Houston. The Magic played tough, and the score was tied after three quarters. But Penny Hardaway missed a last desperation shot at the buzzer as Houston won its third straight game, 106–103.

Shaq wasn't ready to give up. "Anything is possible. We have to believe," he said. But no team had ever come back from a three-games-to-none deficit to win a title. After leading 78–77 in the fourth quarter of Game 4, the Magic gave up control to the Rockets. Houston went on an 11–2 scoring spree, and Orlando had no chance the rest of the way.

Shaq had 25 points, but the Rockets won, 113–101, to take the series and title. As they celebrated, Orlando Coach Brian Hill made his team stay on the floor and watch the party as a motivation for the future.

Shaq cried. This is what he said to reporters: "We are a young team, and I am a young player. We have nothing to be ashamed of."

They certainly didn't, Shaq most of all. Playing against the center he believes is the best in the league, Shaq held his own, averaging 28 points per game.

"Believe me, their day will come," Houston Coach Rudy Tomjanovich said of the Magic. "And it will come soon."

8

Hello, L.A.

Everyone thought Orlando would win an NBA title soon. Shaq was getting better with each game. Penny Hardaway was dishing out assists and scoring from all over the court. The team looked like a dynasty in the making. But, sometimes, things just don't work out the way they're supposed to.

Things definitely did *not* work out during Shaq's fourth season in Orlando.

Early on, Shaq was injured. He missed the first 22 games of the season. That certainly wasn't supposed to happen. Even in Shaq's absence, though, the Magic went on an amazing 17–5 run, thanks to the stellar play of Penny. For his efforts, Penny was named NBA Player of the Month in November.

When Shaq did return, the big guy didn't miss a beat. He finished the season on a roll. He was third in the league in scoring (26.6 points a game), third in field-goal percentage (.573), and ninth in blocked shots (2.13).

The Magic won 60 games for the first time in its

history. It headed into the post-season looking about as stoppable as a speeding freight train.

Despite appearances, all was not well with the Magic. Shaq and Penny (who had become a star in his own right) were not getting along. Both were young and talented and found it difficult to share the spotlight. Although they — and the rest of their teammates — were playing well, they didn't have the mental attitude or toughness to beat the best team in the NBA. Unfortunately, that is exactly who they met in the Eastern Conference Finals: the amazing Chicago Bulls.

Chicago was coming off the best run in NBA history, a 72–10 regular season. Michael Jordan, Scottie Pippen, and Dennis Rodman were hitting on all cylinders. It didn't help that the Magic had spoiled Michael's return to the NBA playoffs the year before by beating the Bulls in the second round of the playoffs. The 1996 Eastern Conference series was set up to be sweet-revenge time for number 23. Michael had been stripped of the ball on a critical possession in the previous year's playoff series against Orlando. He remembered that play.

And he didn't like it.

The Bulls swept Orlando in four games. They won by an average of 16.8 points! Neither Shaq nor Penny could get anything started against Chicago's outstanding defense. Dennis Rodman, one of the greatest rebounders in NBA history, controlled the boards, and Scottie Pippen dominated inside *and* outside. In addition, Horace Grant, a key rebounding presence in the Magic lineup, played only one game of the series because of an elbow injury. That didn't help Orlando's cause.

The 1995-96 season had started with so much promise. Now, it ended with another painful series sweep. It marked the third straight time the Magic had been swept out of the playoffs to end the season.

Shaq wasn't happy for a lot of reasons. There was the loss to Chicago. He and Penny were still having their problems. Then there was the continuing criticism by the media that he didn't work hard enough on his game.

Shaq's contract with the Magic was up after the season. He decided it was time for a change of scenery. What a change he made! On July 18, 1996, Shaquille signed a free-agent contract with the Los Angeles Lakers worth $120 million.

The deal moved him 2,500 miles away from Orlando. It propelled him into the elite group of great centers who had played for the Lakers — George Mikan, Wilt Chamberlain, and Kareem Abdul-Jabbar. All three of them had led the Lakers to championships and earned places in the Basketball Hall of Fame. Surely Shaq would follow in their footsteps!

Before playing for the Lakers, though, Shaquille played for another famous team, Dream Team II. As the starting center for the U.S. men's basketball team at the 1996 Summer Olympics, Shaq helped lead the U.S. to a gold medal in Atlanta, Georgia.

When the Lakers' season started, the newest Laker made quite an impact. He missed 31 games with knee and ankle injuries, but in the 51 games he did play, Los Angeles had an outstanding 38–13 record. He helped the Lakers advance to the second round of the playoffs. In Game 1 of the first round, Shaq scored 46 points against the Portland Trail Blazers. That was the highest single-game playoff output by a Laker since Jerry West scored 53 points against the Boston Celtics, in 1969.

But even Shaq couldn't overcome the powerful and experienced Utah Jazz. The Jazz beat Los Angeles, four games to one, in the Western Conference semi-finals.

Shaq jumped off to a tremendous start in his second season in Los Angeles. The Lakers began the 1997-98 season with 11 straight victories before Shaquille hurt himself again. This time it was an injured stomach muscle, and he missed 21 games.

The Lakers missed Shaq, but they were lucky to have three rising stars. Second-year guard Kobe Bryant, sharpshooting point guard Nick Van Exel, and swingman Eddie Jones carried the load while Shaq was out. Kobe, Nick, Eddie, and Shaquille all played for the Western Conference in the All-Star Game, marking the first time in 15 seasons that four players from the same team had appeared in the mid-season game.

Shaq averaged 28.3 points per game to finish the season second only to Michael Jordan in scoring. He also averaged 11.4 rebounds and led the league with a 58.4 field-goal percentage. In the playoffs, though, Utah again awaited. This time the Jazz and Lakers met in the Western Conference Finals. The results were too similar to the previous year for Laker fans. Utah swept L.A., four games to none. Once again, Shaq missed making it to the NBA Finals and a shot at the league championship!

Laker fans were growing impatient for a title. They almost didn't get a *season* in 1998–99. A disagreement between the NBA owners and the players association over contracts cost the league 32 games of the season.

When the gates opened and the games began, the Lakers played well, compiling a 31–19 record. Shaquille averaged 26.3 points per game and was just barely edged out of the scoring title by guard Allen Iverson of the Philadelphia 76ers. (Allen scored 26.8 points per game.)

That season's playoff exit was different only because it was not the Utah Jazz who showed the Lakers the door. This time, the San Antonio Spurs did the honors. The Spurs beat L.A. in four straight games in the second round and went on to win the championship.

In three seasons in California, Shaq had played some of the best basketball of his career. However, playoff glory still eluded him. The rumblings were getting louder from fans and reporters: Could Shaquille O'Neal win a championship?

9
Ring of Champions

Shaquille began the 1999–2000 NBA season surrounded by a sea of doubts. There were questions about his work ethic. Many reporters and fans believed Shaq spent too much time recording rap albums and making movies instead of working at basketball. In Los Angeles, which is just minutes from Hollywood, Shaquille had more distractions from basketball than ever before.

There were questions about his poor free-throw shooting from the time Shaq entered the NBA. Many teams adopted the "Hack-a-Shaq" method of defense to take advantage of his struggles at the line. Teams would swarm him, hoping he would either commit a foul, or get fouled himself and have to shoot free throws. Often, the strategy worked, as Shaq could rarely make two free throws in a row. Shaquille hadn't been able to improve his free-throw shooting at all. He shot 59 percent from the line his rookie year, and he shot 54 percent seven seasons later, in the 1998-99 season.

There were also questions about the Lakers as a team. Could the talented Kobe become a consistent star? Could the whole team play tough defense for an entire game or series? Clearly, the Lakers had the talent to win a title but, because of all these questions, they were tabbed the most underachieving team in the NBA. The Lakers needed to shake that rap, and Shaq needed to prove that he was a winner.

Laker executive vice president Jerry West made a big move to try to answer all of the question marks: He hired Phil Jackson as head coach. Coach Jackson had won six world championships with the Chicago Bulls. He had led the Bulls to the best-ever record in NBA history (72–10) and produced what many believe is the greatest sports dynasty of the 1990's.

Of course, he had a pretty good team to coach in Chicago. But the Bulls had struggled to find success in the playoffs until Coach Jackson became their coach. He had helped them get over that hurdle. Could he do the same thing for the Lakers?

First, Coach Jackson turned his attention to Shaq. He loved the big fella's game, but thought there was plenty of untapped potential in his mammoth 7' 1" body. In setting up the team's offense, Coach Jackson put Shaq in the most important role on the court. It would be Shaquille's decision-making skills on offense that would make or break the Lakers. With so many teams going to the swarming "Hack-a-Shaq" method, Shaq would now be asked to pass quickly out of double-teams to find the open man.

When the season began, Shaq immediately found himself on the spot. Kobe had injured his hand and was lost for the first 15 games. Shaq had to take control offensively *and* defensively. The Lakers jumped on his broad shoulders to take the ride of their lives.

Throughout the season, Shaq was clearly the best player on his team and in the entire league. Even after Kobe returned to the starting lineup, Shaq dominated. At the All-Star Game, he was named the co-MVP after a 22-point, nine-rebound effort. He was named the NBA's Player of the Month in November, February, and March.

This time, Shaq won the scoring title — his second — with a spectacular 29.7 points-per-game average. He finished second in rebounds, with 13.6 boards a game, and was the third-best shot blocker in basketball, with 3.03 blocks per game. Shaquille also led the league in field-goal percentage at .574, and had 3.8 assists per game. That's a lot of assists for a center, and it showed that he had used wisely that decision-making role Coach Jackson gave him.

With Shaq dominating the inside against every team in the league, Kobe was able to produce his best season, too. Other key contributors were forward Robert Horry

[OR-ee], forward Glen Rice, forward Rick Fox, and guard Derek Fisher. The Lakers steamrolled over the Western Conference, winning 67 of 82 regular-season games and easily clinching home-court advantage throughout the playoffs. Most NBA watchers were ready to hand Los Angeles the NBA title on a silver platter.

But not so fast.

After all, this was the same team that had been swept from the playoffs the previous two seasons. With the exception of Robert Horry, the biggest stars had never won an NBA championship. Robert had played on the Houston Rockets' championship teams in 1994 and 1995, but that seemed like a long time ago. Despite their outstanding season, the Lakers still had something to prove.

In the first round of the playoffs, the Lakers played the unpredictable Sacramento Kings. Led by the versatile Chris Webber and flashy point guard Jason Williams, the Kings tested the Lakers more than most thought possible. Whenever the Kings made a serious charge, though, Shaq stopped them with a thundering dunk or a sweet mini-hook shot from the paint. His 46 points and 17 rebounds in Game 1 set the tone. L.A. won that game and the next. After losing Games 3 and 4 in Sacramento, the Lakers thumped the Kings in the fifth game, 113–86, behind another dominating performance from Shaq (32 points, 18 boards) to win the series.

Shaquille was only getting started. In the Lakers'

Shaquille was too much for Indiana in the NBA Finals.

second series, against the Phoenix Suns, he immediately informed the undersized Suns that this was his game, his playoffs, and his world championship trophy. He opened the series with 37 points and 14 rebounds in a decisive 105–77 victory. Phoenix managed to steal one game, but Los Angeles cruised to the next round with a 4–1 series victory. Shaq scored 37, 38, and 37 points in the first three games.

In the Western Conference Finals, it was time to face

the Portland Trail Blazers again. Shaquille again sent a firm message in Game 1 with 41 points, 11 rebounds, and 7 assists in a 109–94 victory.

But the Trail Blazers were not about to go down that easily. Portland rocked L.A.'s STAPLES Center in Game 2 with a shocking 106–77 victory over the Lakers. Shaq was double- and triple-teamed: He scored just 23 points. The Lakers returned the favor in Games 3 and 4 in Portland as they won both contests to take a 3–1 series lead. The series was now going back to Los Angeles.

Then something strange happened: The Trail Blazers tied the series! They won at STAPLES, 96–88, and then took Game 6 on their home court, 103–93. The season would come down to one game, in Los Angeles.

Forward Rasheed Wallace played a magnificent series for the Trail Blazers. Scottie Pippen, the former Bull star, Steve Smith, and Damon Stoudamire were all rock solid too. Midway through Game 7, in Los Angeles, Rasheed looked like the series MVP. Portland was dominating the game on the Lakers' home court. Shaq was struggling, Kobe couldn't find enough shots, and the rest of the Lakers were being outplayed by the quicker and more aggressive Trail Blazers. At the end of the third quarter, Portland led 71–58.

Clearly, for the Lakers — and for Shaq — it was now

or never. Eight seasons without a championship were simply too many for Shaq to take. He chose *now!*

In one of the all-time great comebacks in NBA history, the Lakers outscored Portland 31-13 in the fourth quarter, and won the game, 89–84. Shaq and Kobe took total control of the game on both ends of the floor. With 11.3 seconds left to play, Shaq dunked a perfectly thrown alley-oop pass from Kobe to ignite the sellout crowd at STAPLES Center and put the finishing touches on an awesome performance. Shaq and the Lakers were heading to the NBA Finals!

"This is what makes champions," Kobe said. "We watched Game 7's growing up all the time, and to finally play in one is a beautiful feeling."

The team's reward was to face the experienced Indiana Pacers for the NBA championship. Pacer veterans such as Reggie Miller, Mark Jackson, and Rik Smits were making their first championship series visit, and they wanted to make the trip count. Pacer head coach Larry Bird was coaching in his last series, so his motivation to win was obvious.

But the Pacers' desire was not enough against an equally motivated Shaquille. In Game 1, the big guy scored 43 points and grabbed 19 rebounds. Los Angeles won 104–87, and Shaq basically established himself as Mount Everest. That challenge proved too much for the pesky Pacers to climb.

Shaq scored 40 and ripped down 24 rebounds in Game

2, as the Lakers won, 111–104. Although Indiana used the "Hack-a-Shaq" strategy, it wasn't enough. Shaquille did miss more than a few free throws (he was 18 of 39 from the line), but the Lakers would not be denied.

Game 3 went to the Pacers despite another solid effort from Shaq (33 points, 13 rebounds). Reggie finally found his long-distance shooting range, and Jalen Rose played a super game as Indiana won, 100–91.

In the best game of the series, Los Angeles won Game 4, in Indiana, 120–118, in overtime. Shaq scored 36 points and grabbed 21 rebounds, but he fouled out with 2:33 left in overtime. It was left to Kobe to make the difference.

The Lakers had a chance to win the title in Game 5, but suffered a letdown and Indiana coasted to a 120–87 blowout. Shaquille played well with 35 points and 11 boards, but his teammates couldn't find their shooting range. And no one could stop the Pacer stars.

When the series returned to Los Angeles for Game 6, the stage was set for another chance to clinch the title. This time, the Lakers didn't disappoint. Shaq scored 41 points, and the Lakers won their 12th NBA championship. Coach Jackson claimed his seventh ring as head coach. And best of all, Shaq finally got his first!

"Shaq's the most dominating player in our league," Coach Bird said. "He's powerful, strong, able to get the ball in the hole. He's improved immensely, starting to make shots further from the basket. He's just so dominating that they have an opportunity here to do something great for a number of years."

Shaq didn't have such nice things to say about his performance. That's "the ugliest forty-one I've ever scored," he said.

Still, tears of joy streamed down his cheeks. At 28 years of age, Shaquille O'Neal finally stood atop the basketball world. He was MVP of the league, MVP of the All-Star Game, and, now — at last — he was MVP of the NBA Finals. Shaquille was the best player on the best team in the best league in the world.

His father's words had come true. It was Shaq's ball, his court, his ring, and his league.